The Magic Mountain

A Guide to Defining and Using a Budget Surplus

Kevin A. Hassett
and R. Glenn Hubbard

The AEI Press

Publisher for the American Enterprise Institute

WASHINGTON, D.C.

1999

Available in the United States from the AEI Press, c/o Publisher Resources Inc., 1224 Heil Quaker Blvd., P.O. Box 7001, La Vergne, TN 37086-7001. Distributed outside the United States by arrangement with Eurospan, 3 Henrietta Street, London WC2E 8LU England.

ISBN 0-8447-7127-9

1 3 5 7 9 10 8 6 4 2

THE AEI PRESS
Publisher for the American Enterprise Institute
1150 17th Street, N.W., Washington, D.C. 20036

Printed in the United States of America

Contents

Acknowledgments

This essay was prepared for discussion at an AEI workshop on April 24, 1998. The authors thank Alex Brill and Elizabeth Cooper Wayt for expert assistance, Daniel Shaviro for comments, and Alan Auerbach, Hans Castorp, Darrel Cohen, Eric Engen, and John Sturrock for helpful advice. The authors also wish to thank Jagadeesh Gokhale for providing data.

1
Introduction

All adults consider how to manage surpluses and deficits in family and business budgets. Whether a budget deficit or surplus makes sense for a family or business depends on what the money does. Borrowing funds for productive investments in education or physical capital does not equate with borrowing for a vacation or a steak dinner. Nor would we view in the same light spending surplus funds to reduce high-interest debt and spending on magazine subscriptions.

For many young adults, talk of a budget surplus for the federal government is something new. After two decades of debates over the evils of federal budget deficits,[1] policymakers and pundits (and even a few economists) are suggesting ways to spend the money. Before labeling a deficit as bad or good, we must ask what the deficit is being used for. Before asking that, we must ask whether a deficit or surplus exists and how large or small it is. In this monograph we first describe the surprising complexity involved in answering such a question, and we present the standard and alternative measures proposed in the literature. We then discuss the shortcomings of even the most sophisticated current measures. Next we discuss several recent policy proposals that suggest ways to spend any potential surplus.

2
Methods of Measuring a Federal Budget Surplus

I n this section we summarize several approaches to measuring the federal budget deficit or surplus. We begin with the method most commonly used by the federal government and then consider several modifications of that traditional approach and a different alternative, generational accounting.

Traditional Method for Measuring the Surplus

The traditional method for measuring the federal budget surplus or deficit is simply to take the difference between current government receipts and current outlays. If receipts in a given year exceed outlays, the budget records a surplus; if outlays over the period exceed receipts, the budget records a deficit:

$$(\text{deficit or surplus})_t = \text{revenues}_t - \text{outlays}_t \quad (2\text{--}1)$$

where t indexes the year.

Such measures of a budget surplus or deficit are motivated by an emphasis on a "national income accounting" view of fiscal policy and by analyses of the effects of the flow of government net borrowing or lending on market interest rates. While intuitive, such measures rely on possibly arbitrary definitions of taxes and spending, confuse oper-

TABLE 2-1

CBO FEDERAL BUDGET SURPLUS ESTIMATE, JANUARY 1999
(dollars in billions)

	1999	2000	2001	2002	2003	2004	2005	2006	2007	2008	2009	Total
Total surplus estimate	107	131	151	209	209	234	256	306	333	355	381	2,672
% of GDP	1.2	1.4	1.6	2.1	2.0	2.2	2.3	2.6	2.7	2.7	2.8	

SOURCE: Congressional Budget office (1999).

3

ating and capital transactions of the government, and ignore changes in the value of government assets and liabilities.[2] While traditional deficit or surplus measures figure prominently in official budget forecasts and in public policy discussions, economists generally argue that those measures are not a reliable guide to the stance of fiscal policy.

Table 2–1 presents the latest deficit projections from the Congressional Budget Office with its traditional approach for measuring the deficit. These figures, released in January 1999, incorporate the latest economic projections. This measurement shows a significant surplus over the next ten years and is the primary motivation of the recent proposals that mention a surplus.

On-Budget Surplus or Deficit. Some tax revenue collected in the current fiscal year may be intended for outlay in future fiscal years. Such revenue generally goes into a trust fund for that purpose; several trust funds exist. The Social Security Trust Fund is perhaps the most visible, but trust funds also exist for Medicare, military retirement, civilian retirement, unemployment, highways, airports and airways, and other purposes. The traditional accounting method subtracts outlays in year t from the total revenues collected in year t (including revenues intended for expenditure in future years) and thereby distorts the current budget deficit or surplus by including revenues not spent in that year. The on-budget deficit is calculated as follows:

(federal funds deficit or surplus)$_t$ = revenues$_t$ − outlays$_t$ − (deposits to trust funds)$_t$. (2–2)

Table 2–2 illustrates the differences between the on-budget, the off-budget, and the traditional deficit or surplus, computed from CBO projections from January 1999. An important result emerges from the two measurement approaches. The traditional approach projects a total budget surplus of $2.672 trillion until the year 2009, while

TABLE 2-2
On-Budget and Off-Budget Components of the Surplus, January 1999
(in billions of dollars)

Projections	1999	2000	2001	2002	2003	2004	2005	2006	2007	2008	2009
Off-budget surplus	127	138	145	153	161	171	183	193	204	212	217
On-budget surplus or deficit	−19	−7	6	55	48	63	72	113	130	−43	164
Revenues	1,815	1,870	1,930	2,015	2,091	2,184	2,288	2,393	2,500	2,611	2,727
Total outlays	1,707	1,739	1,779	1,806	1,881	1,951	2,032	2,086	2,166	2,255	2,346
Traditional surplus estimate[a]	107	131	151	209	209	234	256	306	333	355	381

a. May differ from revenues − total outlays because of rounding.
Source: Congressional Budget Office (1999).

5

the on-budget approach projects a total surplus of $768 billion. The huge projected budget surpluses of the next ten years are reduced by more than 70 percent after accounting for the future expenditures of the Social Security and other trust funds.

Current Account Method

As discussed in chapter 1, not all spending is the same. The current account method distinguishes between government spending on consumption or transfers such as Social Security payments and spending on capital investment such as highway maintenance. To return to the example of the family, when a family borrows $200,000 to purchase a home, its assets and liabilities both go up by $200,000, and its net worth remains unchanged. If, however, a family can borrow without collateral and then give the borrowed money to a friend, its liability increases, but its assets do not. Similarly, if the government borrows to build a highway, assets and liabilities should cancel. But if funds are borrowed and transferred to particular groups in society, the action does not create any capital assets.

Some economists have suggested calculating the budget deficit or surplus to reflect these facts by distinguishing between current spending and capital spending. With this approach the budget deficit or surplus would equal

$$(\text{deficit or surplus}) = (\text{revenues}) - (\text{current noncapital spending}) - (\text{depreciation of capital stock}). \quad (2\text{–}3)$$

The principal difficulty in this approach is determining current spending and capital spending. Some items (such as infrastructure projects) are easy to categorize, while others—for example, investment in human capital (educational services)—are trickier. Eisner (1986) estimates that if the federal government used a current account method to calculate the deficit or surplus, the deficit would then be 30–50 percent lower.

Federal Regulation and State and Local Government Spending. Federal regulations can force individuals and corporations to spend funds in ways that do not end up in the coffers of the Treasury Department. New clean air regulations that require firms to install scrubbers in their smokestacks exemplify this well. Traditional measures of fiscal stance do not include any accounting of liabilities associated with changes in regulations, though in principle they should.

The Office of Management and Budget (1998b), for example, calculated the total regulatory cost for the year 1998 as $170–224 billion. A regulatory optimist would presume a benefit-cost ratio of greater than unity while a pessimist would presume a benefit-cost ratio closer to zero.

The federal government can also shift the burden of a program to the state or local level without providing funding for the program and thereby reduce federal outlays but force other forms of government to finance these programs (through either increased taxes or borrowing). Discussion of the "crowding out" effect of government debt, particularly on raising the cost of borrowing for all debtors, should include this fiscal shift.

Full-Employment Measurement. In addition to using the traditional method to report the deficit and surplus, the CBO has also measured the budget deficit on the assumption of an unemployment rate consistent with stable inflation, that is, the nonaccelerating inflation rate of unemployment (NAIRU). This rate is currently estimated as 5.6 percent, down from 5.9 percent in 1990 and 6.2 percent in 1980. This method of calculation estimates what the deficit or surplus would have been had the economy been at full employment. This approach can be useful for comparing changes in budgets over time. Table 2–3 shows both the full employment deficit and the traditional deficit in dollar terms and as a percent of the gross domestic product.

TABLE 2–3
TRADITIONAL BUDGET DEFICIT AND FULL EMPLOYMENT
BUDGET DEFICIT, 1975–1998

	1975	1980	1985	1990	1995	1998
Traditional budget deficit (billions of dollars)	–53	–74	–212	–221	–164	70
Full employment budget deficit (billions of dollars)	–37	–63	–196	–183	–187	–1
Traditional budget deficit (% of GDP)	–3.4	–2.7	–5.2	–3.9	–2.3	0.8
Full employment budget deficit (as a % of GDP)	–2.3	–2.3	–4.7	–3.2	–2.6	0.0
NAIRU[a]	6.2	6.2	6.0	5.9	5.6	5.6

a. Nonaccelerating inflation rate of unemployment.
SOURCE: Congressional Budget Office (1999).

Until 1995 the actual deficit (as determined by the traditional method) exceeded the full-employment deficit. Since 1995, the full-employment deficit has been larger because the U.S. economy is operating at an unemployment rate below the NAIRU. Although this status suggests inflationary pressure on the economy, such pressure is not evident. The rate of inflation has averaged 2.3 percent per year since 1995, and for the past twelve months, the consumer price index has increased by just 1.6 percent. A cautionary note: this approach can only be as accurate as the NAIRU.

Generational Accounting

Auerbach and Kotlikoff (1987); Kotlikoff (1992,1993); Auerbach, Gokhale, and Kotlikoff (1991, 1992); and

Auerbach (1994) have emphasized that the simple adding up of current receipts and expenditures provides little information about the major concern: the change in the government's assets and liabilities. If, for example, the government suspended all Social Security spending but promised to triple it the next year, then this year's budget would benefit, even though future liabilities would be much greater. As Auerbach and Kotlikoff emphasized, short-term measures ignore described future policy. Furthermore, a simple deficit measure does not consider the intergenerational distribution of the burden of government spending.

A meaningful measure of the surplus should convey the concept that what we do today affects what is required of us tomorrow. Launching a new entitlement program that is likely to become politically entrenched should have a different effect on a measurement of surplus than a one-time expenditure to address the damage caused by a hurricane. Auerbach and Kotlikoff developed generational accounting, a method of calculating the government surplus that indicates what, in present value, a typical member of each age cohort should expect to pay the government, on net, now and in the future. They begin with a deceptively simple formula, which describes the intertemporal government budget constraint:

$$PVT_{\text{current gen.}} + PVT_{\text{future gen.}} = PVG - GW \qquad (2\text{--}4)$$

where PVT is the present value of all taxes paid by the current and future generations, PVG is the present value of all future government consumption, and GW is government net wealth. Generational accounts are a set of PVTs for current and future generations that, when added up, represent enough funds to balance exactly PVG – GW. Given a path of tax rates, government spending, and an expected lifetime for a cohort member, one could calculate the tax burden for a cohort representative over that individual's lifetime and how this figure compares with the "consumption" of government over that lifetime. Any residual would have to be paid by future generations and would therefore be included in $\text{PVT}_{\text{future gen.}}$. The economic content of any policy changes can, at least in part, be tracked in a much better way by generational accounting because this approach identifies, given a set of assumptions, exactly how fiscal policies alter what current and future generations can be expected to pay in taxes over their lifetimes.

When economists present both a traditional way and a better way to look at a question, sometimes the traditional way reflects policymakers' view of the world, and the better way, something that those policymakers are hesitant to embrace. Happily, this is not the case here. The Office of Management and Budget published generational accounts in the 1993 and 1994 budgets, and staff economists of the Congressional Budget Office are at the forefront of research into generational accounting.

Because government liabilities are extremely backloaded and extend beyond the time frame of our earlier tables, generational accounting methods tell a much different story than traditional forecasts. Gokhale, Page, and Sturrock (1999) calculate the $\text{PVT}_{\text{current gen.}}$ (with 1995 as the base year) at $22.1 trillion (1995 dollars) and $\text{PVT}_{\text{future gen.}}$ (for those born in 1996 or after) at $9.4 trillion. ($\text{PVT}_{\text{future gen.}}$ is discounted to 1995 dollars.) These figures can be equated to a lifetime net tax rate of 28.6 percent for individuals born in 1995 but a tax rate of 49.2 percent for future generations.[3] Generational accounting exposes the fiscal imbalance of this greater burden on future generations. Under the assumptions used here, the degree of imbalance is 71.9 percent.[4]

3
Problems with Budget Projections

Some Common Issues

Regardless of the method of measuring the surplus, serious technical and conceptual issues arise. Below we discuss some problems with the different methods.

Some problems are common to any measurement method. First, economists cannot predict changes in government policy. Therefore, one must generally assume that taxing and spending will continue as currently planned. This is a major assumption. The most detailed budget deficit projections made during the final year of the Carter administration, for example, could not possibly have anticipated the spending increases and the tax cuts of the Reagan administration.

Second, all budget projections are sensitive to economic conditions such as the growth rate of the economy's output, the inflation rate, and the unemployment rate. The CBO overestimated the budget deficit for five years in a row, primarily because of stronger-than-expected economic growth and lower-than-expected unemployment and inflation.

Even in the short run, making deficit and surplus projections is difficult. In January 1998 the CBO projected the cumulative surplus from 1998 through 2008 at $655 billion. In March 1998 that number was revised to $679 billion, and in July 1998 the CBO was projecting a surplus of $1.611 trillion. Finally, CBO's latest estimates, from January 1999, project the ten-year surplus to total $2.672 trillion. In a one-year period the total ten-year budget surplus projection has increased from 40 percent to more than 160 percent of the 1998 federal budget.

For twenty-nine years, until 1998, we experienced federal budget deficits. By contrast, in 1960 the budget was nearly balanced, with approximately one-tenth of a percent of GDP in surplus, or less than $500 million. Since 1956 the federal budget had surplus only in four years; it has had a deficit for thirty-eight years, including every year since 1969. (These numbers include funds earmarked to trust funds.)

All current talk about surpluses has emanated from surpluses projected by the Congressional Budget Office. The CBO has never perfectly estimated the budget deficit or surplus. Fiscal year 1998 was the sixth straight year in which the actual deficit was less than that anticipated by the budget resolution. This situation may just reflect unbelievably good fortune; Auerbach (1994) has developed several political economy arguments to explain an upward bias to official revenue forecasts. Before fiscal year 1993 the actual deficit exceeded the target in the budget resolution for thirteen consecutive years. Over the entire period the difference between budget resolution targets and actual deficits has ranged from less than 1 percent to more than 11 percent of actual outlays. In this respect 1983 was the worst year since 1980, with the CBO underestimating the deficit by 11.4 percent of GDP. The next year, 1984, was the CBO's best forecasting year since 1980, with the actual deficit a mere 0.5 percent greater than the estimated deficit. In 1997 the CBO overestimated the FY1997 deficit by 8.2 percent. Reasons for the error point toward underestimates in the performance of the economy. At the beginning of the fiscal year, the CBO projected a real GDP growth rate of 2.0 percent, while actual growth was 3.7 percent. CBO predicted unemployment would be 6.0 percent, but the rate was actually 5.1 percent. Finally, the projection of the inflation rate (measured by the change in the consumer price index for all urban consumers) was 3.1 percent, while the actual rate was only 2.7 percent.

Generational accounting is also sensitive to changes in demographic and economic projections. The basic case described above assumes a long-term growth rate of productivity of 1.2 percent and a discount rate of 6 percent. As mentioned, Gokhale, Page, and Sturrock (1999) calculate the difference in lifetime net taxes between current newborns and future generations at 72 percent. With a discount rate of 9 percent, the difference jumps to 130 percent; with a discount rate of just 3 percent, the difference shrinks to 53 percent. Likewise, a higher growth rate of productivity of 1.7 percent lessens the burden to 55 percent more for future generations. Conversely, a slower productivity growth rate of just 0.7 percent will give future generations a lifetime net tax burden 88 percent greater than that of current newborns.

The setup for generational accounting has lessened the burden on future generations in the past few years. Lifetime net tax rates for newborns and future generations calculated with 1993 as the base year instead of 1995 were 34.2 and 84.4 percent, respectively, with the degree of imbalance at 147.1 percent. Today's imbalance is half that.

A Look at the Longer Term in the Traditional View

While the traditional near-term outlook shows a surplus, the long-run aging of the U.S. population and the decline in the number of workers per person covered by Social Security put tremendous pressure on government's long-run finances. Table 3–1 presents estimates of the long-

TABLE 3–1
Long-Run Budget Deficit Projections
(as a percentage of GDP)

Assumptions	1995	2000	2005	2010	2020	2030	2040	2050	2060	2070
With current policy assumptions	0.09	2.7	3.0	3.3	1.8	0.03	–0.2	–0.9	–2.4	–4.3
With continued rapid Medicare growth[a]	0.09	2.7	3.0	3.3	1.6	–0.5	–1.6	–3.4	–6.2	–9.3
With discretionary spending growing with population	0.09	2.7	3.0	3.2	1.5	–0.2	0.7	–1.5	2.9	–4.8

a. The Health Care Financing Administration is projecting a slowdown in Medicare costs around 2020. If this slowdown does not occur, the budget deficit will increase significantly.

Source: Office of Management and Budget (1998a).

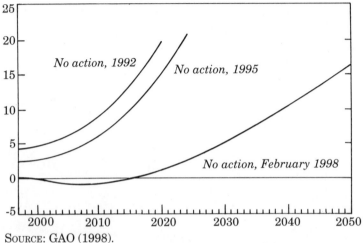

FIGURE 3–1
GAO LONG-RUN FEDERAL SURPLUS PROJECTIONS,
1992, 1995, AND 1998
(percent of GDP)

SOURCE: GAO (1998).

run budget projections from *Analytical Perspectives 1998*, a supplement to the federal budget. These projections, provided under several assumptions, contain the most recent available long-run OMB projections.

As the table indicates, the aging of the population takes a serious toll on government finances toward the middle of the next century. If the growth of Medicare expenditures does not slow, the deficit will, all else being equal, climb to 9.3 percent of GDP; even given some restraint on this growth, the deficit climbs to 4–5 percent of GDP.

Despite these still substantial deficits, positive recent events have improved the long-run picture. Figure 3–1, taken from testimony from Paul Posner of the Government Accounting Office (GAO 1998), sheds some light on this. Figure 3–1 plots the long-run path of the government surplus in the 1992, 1995, and 1998 long-run forecasts by GAO. In 1992 the total deficit for 1997 was projected to be almost 5 percent of GDP. In 1995 the 1997 deficit was fore-cast at about 2.5 percent of GDP. In fact, the federal bud-get almost balanced. Both previous forecasts had projected the deficit to climb higher than 15 percent of GDP in the succeeding twenty years. Under the current projection, the deficit does not return to the level previously forecast for 1997 until about 2030.

Unsurprisingly, the longer-term view looks more like that in the generational accounts. The generational ac-counts pull forward future liabilities and clarify the real current budgetary impact of new future liabilities.

4
What Does a Surplus Mean?

Ricardian Equivalence

Robert Barro (1974, 1989) has argued that under certain assumptions the issuance of government debt has no impact on the economy. Because the government must adhere to a long-run budget constraint, his model considers a deficit at any time as just a signal of the timing of liabilities. Today's high deficit means that tomorrow's taxes must be higher, and individuals will recognize this and adjust their spending plans accordingly. This statement clearly requires some strong assumptions; most notably, individuals must be rational and face perfect capital markets, and government taxes must be a lump sum and hence nondistortionary.

If Barro were correct, we should have seen an increase in household saving while government debt increased to finance current consumption-boosting transfer programs such as social security (Gramlich 1989). We have not seen such a savings path— in fact we have seen the reverse. Government debt likely has some real consequences. Other factors may affect the saving rate, but Bernheim (1990) showed that even after other factors had been considered, savings did not offset debt. Intergenerational altruism may exist, but no empirical evidence suggests that government debt can be ignored.

Although generational accounts are useful measures of the effects of different government policies on the welfare of future generations, they implicitly involve two assumptions—and this aspect is often ignored. First, the Ricardian equivalence does not hold. If it did, then parental altruism would simply adjust current saving in response to changing generational liabilities so that the net effect of different policies on future generations would be zero (or at least muted significantly). The second related assumption is that changes in government policy alter the stock of wealth left for future generations. We explore next whether ignoring this change in wealth materially affects conclusions suggested by generational accounts.

The Effect of Government Policy on Future Generations

While generational accounts provide a more accurate measure of the narrowly focused budgetary impact of policy changes than the traditional method does, they may not present as complete a picture as one would like.[5] Ricardian equivalence provides one reason, but there are others. Consider the case of an investment tax credit. If the credit increases the marginal return on new capital, then it may increase private saving (at the expense of private consumption) and investment but decrease government revenue. Tomorrow's generations might be better off because they would inherit some fraction of the capital that is accumulated because of the credit, yet both the traditional method and generational accounting would show that future generations are worse off. To take a more extreme example, if an increase in defense spending has a large negative effect on the probability that the country is destroyed, then future generations will be happy that we made the investment, even though both accounting methods will suggest that the spending worsened the financial lot of future generations.

The measurement issues associated with generational accounting are certainly demanding, and those that would account for such effects would probably be more so. Nonetheless, in principle a "best" measure of the impact of government on current and future generations would account for government's various interactions with the livelihood and legacy of our citizens and show the effects of any sequence of policies on total net worth.

Suppose that we were to examine the effects of lowering the corporate tax rate in an open economy where capital is expensed. In such an economy the corporate income tax is just a tax on distributions and has no effect on the marginal decisions of firms financing investment with retained earnings. If the corporate tax were capitalized into equity values, the decline in the corporate tax rate would increase the value of the firm but have, *ceteris paribus*, no effect on the path of capital formation. In this case even a measure of this policy based on generational accounts would say that future generations have been made worse off by the policy because current revenues would decline but current expenditures would not change. This conclusion is not correct, however, because the increase in the value of firms exactly offsets the decline in tax revenues. An infant waking up tomorrow and inheriting this new bundle of policies would be indifferent between it and the alternative with higher corporate tax rates. In principle, then, the neglect of general equilibrium forces may be as serious a drawback for generational accounting as those presented by the traditional flow measures of the surplus.

One back-of-the-envelope solution to this problem would be to augment the generational account net tax numbers with some measure of the net worth inherited by tomorrow's generations (see, for example, Bradford's [1991] concept of market-value savings). Because the current market value of an asset includes the properly discounted net flow of future revenues or services, it should contain

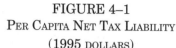

FIGURE 4–1
PER CAPITA NET TAX LIABILITY
(1995 DOLLARS)

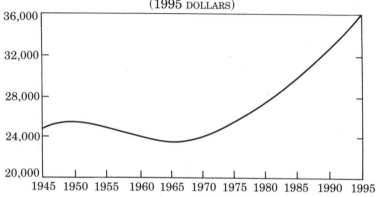

SOURCE: Jagadeesh Gokhale.

the net effects of future liabilities. One problem with this concept as a measure of the current generation's legacy is that some of these assets will necessarily be consumed in old age and depreciation will reduce their value as well. In a work in progress, we are exploring how corrections for these offsets affect the results. But one might consider a simplified "changing of the guard" world in which today's net worth, net of all generational accounts, is handed tomorrow to all future generations. These numbers might help us to assess whether the net stake that today's adults are leaving their progeny is effectively a rotten egg and also to evaluate whether the impact of the large pending liabilities is great enough to outweigh the enormous gains in private wealth that have been achieved.

Figure 4–1 shows the growth of the aggregate per capita tax liability left to future generations, assuming perfect foresight, for the postwar period. The per capita net tax liability went down slightly from 1950 to 1965 ($25,000 to $23,500) and then up steadily to $36,000. As seen in figure 4–2, per capita net worth has grown from

FIGURE 4–2
PER CAPITA NET WEALTH AND NET FUTURE TAX
LIABILITY, 1945–1995
(1995 DOLLARS)

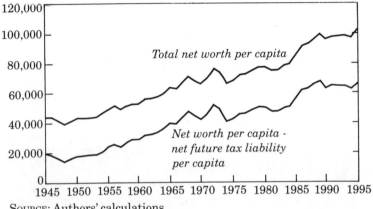

SOURCE: Authors' calculations.

$49,000 to $104,000 over the same period. Because net assets have grown faster than the net tax liability, future generations may still be wealthier than previous generations, according to this simple calculation.

5

What Should We Do If
There Is a Budget Surplus?

We now consider five possible policy options for
dealing with a budget surplus if one should actually occur. They are do nothing, increase
spending, cut taxes, finance fundamental tax reform, and
finance Social Security reform.

Do Nothing (Pay Down the Debt)

"Do nothing" refers to a strategy of maintaining current
federal tax and expenditure policies and thereby using
budget surpluses to reduce government borrowing (or in
principle to reduce levels of government debt). Such a strategy offers two potential benefits. First, it would reduce
the debt burdens of future generations and would miti-
gate the current levels of intergenerational redistribution.
Second, because the United States is not a small, open
economy, reductions in federal borrowing would likely reduce market interest rates.[6] Reductions in market interest rates, in turn, would lower interest rates for consumers
(for example, for home mortgages), for businesses (for example, for fixed investment), and for the federal government (for example, reduced interest outlays).

A Concord Coalition survey of 451 voters asked, "What
percentage of any federal budget surplus should be used

TABLE 5–1
PUBLIC OPINION ON DISPOSITION OF A FEDERAL BUDGET
SURPLUS, FEBRUARY 1998
(in percent)

Option	Portion of Surplus
Pay down the debt	54.6
Reform the tax system	11.4
Finance Social Security transition	10.7
Increase infrastructure spending	8.2
Increase spending on children	7.3
Cut taxes	7.3
Other	0.6

SOURCE: Concord Coalition (1998).

to fund [the following] possible programs?" Table 5–1 tabulates the results. Respondents allocated 54.6 percent of a surplus to "paying down the debt," nearly five times as much as the second most popular option, "reform the tax system." When the survey results are viewed by the age of the respondent, "pay down the debt" is most popular among people aged sixty-five and older, with this group allocating 59.1 percent of any surplus to this option. When the respondents are categorized by income level, those in the lowest third of the income range most favor "paying down the debt," at allocations 62.5 percent of that group.

One sometimes hears the argument—as in a recent proposal by Representative Mark Neumann (R-Wisconsin)—that using surpluses to pay down debt is economically meaningless: such a move is unnecessary because the national debt has essentially no net impact on future generations. Because the debt is just a measure of what current taxpayers owe current bondholders, as the argument goes, it is just a tally of what one group of Americans has borrowed from another and hence has no intergenerational consequences. Washington policy circles have paid attention to this "debt irrelevance" view despite its obvious faults.

A simple example illustrates the problem with this idea. Suppose your parents have some wealth to leave you. What effect would it have on your inheritance if your father borrowed $10,000 from your mother? While you would inherit both your mother's asset and your father's liability, the real effect on your inheritance depends on how the transaction changes what happens to the money. Suppose that your mother always saves every penny, while your father, a gambler, takes the money to the racetrack and loses it. Your inheritance goes down by $10,000, even though the immediate "balance sheet" effect of the loan is a wash. Conversely, if your father is a brilliant stock analyst while your mother always invests in certificates of deposit, your inheritance could go up because of the transaction. Your dad will pay off the IOU when his stock appreciates enough, and anything left over may well go to you when your parents die. Aggregate family debt says nothing about how an inheritance is doing.

The potential benefits of debt reduction or lower federal borrowing, however, are not without "political economy" concerns. Some analysts have argued that budget surpluses might loosen constraints on federal spending. To the extent that such spending (on government transfers or consumption) is inefficient, "benefits" from a surplus would not materialize.[7]

Increase Federal Spending

Consider two countries, one with a national debt of $1,000 per citizen and another with a national debt of $100,000 per citizen. Which country is the better place to be a newborn? The answer depends on what the governments have been doing with the money. If the second country used the money to invest heavily in projects with high returns while the first used the money to subsidize consumption, then you might prefer to inherit the $100,000 debt.

To the extent that the size of the federal government—in terms of government consumption, investment, or transfers—is suboptimally small, surplus funds could be used to increase spending. From the perspective of economic analysis, such a change requires two steps: (1) a reasoned argument that the size of government is too low and (2) proper benefit-cost examination of the spending change (as with the family or business, spending on consumption and on investments must be distinguished). Within the second step, one must incorporate the deadweight loss of raising revenue because the opportunity cost of the funds is their alternative use in current or future tax reduction.

From the perspective of the political economy of the budget process, reasoned analysis of new spending alternatives seems unlikely. President Clinton's most recent budget submission proposes spending about half the total surplus projected by the Congressional Budget Office over the next four years. These proposals include several initiatives in health, education, child care, transportation, school construction, and the environment that do not appear to contain meaningful benefit-cost analysis.

Reduce Federal Taxes

Most tax instruments unavoidably distort the decisions of households as workers or savers and the decisions of firms as employers or investors. Short of relying on pure rent (for example, basketball players' salaries) or on lump-sum taxes generally (for example, a poll tax), taxes generate deadweight loss as well as revenue. The deadweight loss of a tax refers to the amount by which households' well-being is reduced in excess of the government revenue raised. What would be the deadweight loss associated with raising an incremental dollar of revenue? Economists have attempted to measure deadweight losses associated with taxes on labor and capital income and have generally concluded that marginal deadweight losses are large. Ballard, Shoven, and Whalley (1985) calculate the marginal efficiency effect of additional taxes at $0.365 per dollar raised; Browning (1987) estimates the efficiency effect as $0.395 per dollar raised; and Bovenberg and Goulder (1996) calculate $0.260 per dollar raised. All these calculations are for all U.S. taxes collectively. Hausman (1981) calculates the marginal efficiency loss from U.S. income taxes at $0.405 per dollar of revenue raised.

From the perspective of the surplus debate, surplus funds could be used to reduce federal income taxes. To be most effective, such reductions should focus on marginal income tax rates and on marginal rates of taxation of capital income in particular. Recent tax debates suggest, however, that outside a political economy of fundamental tax reform, tax reductions might center on changes with negligible impact on the deadweight loss of the tax system (for example, involving child tax credits or the Hope scholarship credits).[8]

Carry Out Fundamental Tax Reform

Many economists believe that fundamental tax reform could significantly increase economic well-being for current and future U.S. households through changes in saving, investment, and the allocation of capital. Recent proposals include fundamental income tax reform (such as the comprehensive business income tax suggested by Department of the Treasury [1992]) and a switch to a federal consumption tax (as in the flat tax of Hall and Rabushka [1983, 1995] or a national sales tax).[9] While even conservatively estimated gains in long-run economic efficiency are large—Auerbach (1996), for example, estimates a 5 percent long-run gain in output per head from a move to the flat tax—transition costs can be substantial. While the magnitude of such transition costs is debatable (see, for example, Hubbard [1997a]), these costs are an important piece of the debate over tax reform. Because some analysts argue that the distribution of transition costs could undermine the chance of achieving long-run gains in economic well-being associated with fundamental tax reform, the use of continuing federal budget surpluses to finance the transition to a new tax system makes the reform more likely.

A few calculations illustrate the relationship between the size of the transition costs and the size of the surplus. Auerbach (1996) estimates that the switch to a Hall-Rabushka tax would cause a 3.6 percent decline in asset prices and a switch to an Armey-Shelby tax, a 6.9 percent drop. According to the Federal Reserve's flow of funds, the aggregate value of corporate equities held by U.S. households is about $8 trillion in current dollars. If one wanted to issue bonds equal to the present value of asset decline experienced by current asset holders (with Auerbach's estimates) to compensate them, the value of these bonds would be $288 billion. Switching to an Armey-Shelby tax would require $552 billion in recognition bonds. Both numbers are smaller than the sum of the estimated surpluses.

Carry Out Social Security Reform

As the debates summarized in the report of the 1994–1996 Advisory Council on Social Security (1997) indicate, economists and policymakers are concerned that the current pay-as-you-go Social Security system reduces capital formation and generational equity. This concern has led to several proposals for transferring a portion of Social Security payroll tax revenues to privately managed individual accounts (see, for example, the discussion in Feldstein [1998]). Another possibility is the use of accumulated Social Security surpluses (and in principle others) to finance transition costs from a pay-as-you-go Social Security system to one relying more heavily on individual accounts.

Transition costs arise in this context because benefits to the current elderly and to soon-to-be retired households are likely to be honored. How large are such transition costs? Such costs could vary. At current levels of debt to the gross domestic product (where debt includes implicit Social Security obligations), one would need an annual flow equal to the gap between the real interest rate and the economy's growth rate times the stock of unfunded Social Security liabilities currently outstanding.

Feldstein and Samwick (1997) discuss the use of "recognition bonds" to exit the current structure of Social Security. The government would issue these bonds to everyone who has paid into the old Social Security system at a level equivalent to the present value of benefits to which each person is so far entitled. Bonds could then be used to purchase an annuity that would begin payments at retirement. According to Feldstein and Samwick,

> if the value of such a recognition bond is calculated by discounting future benefits at the same rate at which the market is willing to sell a single-premium annuity, the recognition bond would permit the individual to receive the same benefits that he or she would get from the existing PAYGO program. (p. 38)

Feldstein and Samwick estimate the total value of these recognition bonds several ways. First, they calculate the bonds on a "backward looking" basis, the accumulated value of past payroll taxes (net of benefits already received). With a 2 percent discount rate (the real rate the Social Security Trust Fund has received), those bonds would be worth $8.09 trillion. With a 4 percent discount rate, these bonds would total $11.26 trillion. The alternative way of calculating the bonds would be "forward looking"—based on net future benefits to which individuals are entitled. With a 2 percent discount rate, these bonds would be worth $11.99 trillion. With a 4 percent discount rate, the results differ noticeably. Under the current system no one can expect a return as high as 4 percent. Therefore, for some individuals (those under thirty-five) the present value of future taxes exceeds the present value of their benefits—negative net Social Security wealth. Because these people would receive no recognition bonds whatsoever, the total value of recognition bonds would come to only $6.99 trillion for the present work force and retirees. Feldstein and Samwick propose financing these bonds with a payroll tax.

As with fundamental tax reform, using budget surpluses for transition costs of Social Security reform would likely win support on grounds of both "economic efficiency" and "political economy." This conclusion has cropped up in the current debate. President Clinton's announced intention to dedicate projected budget surpluses to Social Security has drawn proposals from Senators Daniel Patrick Moynihan (D-New York) and William V. Roth Jr. (R-Delaware) on the Senate Finance Committee; Senators Phil Gramm (R-Texas), Judd Gregg (R-New Hampshire), and Bob Kerrey (D-Nebraska); Representative Bill Archer (R-Texas), chairman of the House Ways and Means Committee; and Representative John R. Kasich (R-Ohio), chairman of the House Budget Committee.

The scale of the task at hand—paying off recognition bonds—is large, however. At an interest rate of 5 percent, the stock of recognition bonds required to compensate existing stakeholders fully would require an annual interest payment of around $500 billion, about the current size of federal discretionary spending.

6

Conclusions

I n this monograph we have reviewed the various estimates of the budget surplus and discussed the conceptual problems that even the most sophisticated
measures employed to date possess. Our analysis leads us
to three main conclusions.

First, a budget surplus would occur—even under
traditional accounting methods—only when trust fund surpluses were combined with on-budget deficits because
funds are being borrowed from the various trust funds.
Second, both the generational-accounts measure and the
longer-run traditional measure suggest that any surplus
would be short-lived. Third, the projected surplus probably exceeds the amount of money needed to cover transition costs related to fundamental tax reform but falls short
of the funds needed to offset transition costs of privatizing
Social Security.

Notes

1. Shaviro (1997) and Graetz (1997) offer fascinating accounts of the deficit debate during this period.

2. These points have been made many times. Some prominent references include Boskin (1982); Boskin, Robinson, and Huber (1987); Eisner (1986, 1988); and Bradford (1991).

3. Because we do not know how the future generations will share this burden, generational accounting assumes that the burden will be split equally on a growth-adjusted basis.

4. The degree of imbalance is calculated as the percentage difference between lifetime net tax rates. For this calculation it is $(0.492 - 0.286)/0.286 = 0.719$.

5. For critical discussions of generational accounting see Cutler (1993), Diamond (1996), and Haveman (1994).

6. This assumes that Ricardian equivalence (as in Barro, 1974) does not hold. For a simple description of competing views of the effect of budget surpluses on interest rates, see Hubbard (1997b, chap. 6).

7. See Becker and Mulligan (1998) for a clever example of this point.

8. It is also important to note that it may be difficult to distinguish tax cuts from spending increases. At first this may seem strange, but consider a $500 tax credit for college tuition. Government would likely describe this as a tax cut, but it could easily be also described as a spending program.

9. Gentry and Hubbard (1997) describe the economic differences between fundamental income tax reform and consumption tax reform for analysis of economic efficiency and distribution. For the sake of simplicity, we omit discussion of hybrid tax reform proposals, such as the USA tax.

References

Advisory Council on Social Security. 1997. *Report of the 1994–1996 Advisory Council on Social Security*. Washington, D.C.: Government Printing Office.

Auerbach, Alan J. 1994. "The U.S. Fiscal Problem: Where We Are, How We Got Here, and Where We're Going." In *NBER: Macroeconomics Annual*, vol. 9, edited by Stanley Fischer and Julio J. Rotenberg. Cambridge: MIT Press

———. 1996. "Tax Reform, Capital Allocation, Efficiency, and Growth." In *Economic Effects of Fundamental Tax Reform*, edited by Henry J. Aaron and William G. Gale. Washington, D.C.: Brookings Institution.

Auerbach, Alan J., Jagadeesh Gokhale, and Laurence J. Kotlikoff. 1991. "Generational Accounts: A Meaningful Alternative to Deficit Accounting." In *Tax Policy and the Economy*, vol. 5., edited by David F. Bradford. Cambridge: MIT Press.

———. 1992. "Generational Accounting: A New Approach to Understanding the Effects of Fiscal Policy of Saving." *Scandinavian Journal of Economics* 94.

Auerbach, Alan J., and Laurence J. Kotlikoff. 1987. *Dynamic Fiscal Policy*. Cambridge: Cambridge University Press.

Ballard, C. L., J. B. Shoven, and J. Whalley. 1985. "General Equilibrium Computations of the Marginal Welfare Costs of Taxes in the United States." *American Economic Review* 75: 128–38.

Barro, Robert J. 1974. "Are Government Bonds Net Wealth?" *Journal of Political Economy* 82.

———. 1989. "The Neoclassical Approach to Fiscal Policy." In *Modern Business Cycle Theory*, edited by Robert J. Barro. Cambridge: Harvard University Press.

Becker, Gary S., and Casey B. Mulligan. 1988. "Deadweight Costs and the Size of Government." NBER Working Paper 6789.

Bernheim, B. Douglas. 1990. "Richardian Equivalence: An Evaluation of Theory and Evidence." In *NBER Macroeconomics Annual,* edited by Stanley Fischer, pp. 263–303. Cambridge: MIT Press.

Boskin, Michael J. 1982. "Federal Government Deficits: Some Myths and Realities." *American Economic Review* 72.

———. 1986. "Theoretical Issues in the Measurement, Evaluation, and Interpretation of Postwar U.S. Saving." In *Savings and Capital Formation,* edited by F. Gerard Adams and Susan M. Wachter. Lexington: Lexington Books.

Boskin, Michael J., Marc S. Robinson, and Alan M. Huber. 1987. "Government Saving, Capital Formation, and Wealth in the United States, 1947–1985." In *The Measurement of Saving, Investment, and Wealth, NBER Studies in Income and Wealth*, vol. 52, edited by Robert E. Lipsey and Helen Stone Tice. Chicago: University of Chicago Press.

Bovenberg, A. L., and L. H. Goulder. 1996. "Optimal Environmental Taxation in the Presence of Other Taxes: General-Equilibrium Analyses." *American Economic Review* 86: 985–1000.

Bradford, David F. 1991. "Market Value versus Financial Accounting Measures of National Savings." In *National Saving and Economic Performance*, edited by B. Douglas Bernheim and John B. Shoven. Chicago: University of Chicago Press.

Browning, E. K. 1987. "On the Marginal Welfare Cost of Taxation." *American Economic Review* 77: 11–23.

Concord Coalition. 1998. "Poll Results: What Should We Do with Any Emerging Surpluses?" Http:// www.concordcoalition.org/federal_budget/surplus_poll results.html.

Congressional Budget Office. 1998a. *The Economic and Budget Outlook: Fiscal Years 1999–2008*. Washington, D.C.: Government Printing Office, January.

———. 1998b. *An Analysis of the President's Budgetary Proposals for Fiscal Year 1999*, Washington, D.C.: Government Printing Office, March.

———. 1998c. *The Economic and Budget Outlook: Fiscal Years 1999–2008: A Preliminary Update*. Washington, D.C.: Government Printing Office, July.

———. 1999. *The Economic and Budget Outlook: Fiscal Years 2000–2009*. Washington, D.C.: Government Printing Office, January.

Crain, W. Mark, and James C. Miller III. 1990. "Budget Process and Spending Growth." *William and Mary Law Review* 31.

Cutler, David. 1993. "Review of *Generational Accounting: Knowing Who Pays, and When, for What We Spend* by

Laurence J. Kotlikoff." *National Tax Journal* 46.

Diamond, Peter. 1996. "Generational Accounts and Generational Balance: An Assessment." *National Tax Journal* 49.

Eisner, Robert. 1986. *How Real Is the Federal Deficit?* New York: Free Press.

————. 1988. "Extended Accounts for National Income and Product." *Journal of Economic Literature* 26 (December): 1611–84.

Feldstein, Martin. 1998. "Savings Grace." *New Republic*, April 6, 1998, pp. 14–16.

Feldstein, Martin, and Andrew Samwick. 1997. *The Economies of Prefunding Social Security and Medicare Benefits*. NBER Working Paper 6055.

Friedman, Benjamin M. 1988. *Day of Reckoning: The Consequences of American Economic Policy under Reagan and After.* New York: Random House.

Gentry, William M., and R. Glenn Hubbard. 1997. "Distributional Implications of Introducing a Broad-Based Consumption Tax." In *Tax Policy and the Economy*, vol. 11, edited by James M. Poterba. Cambridge: MIT Press.

————. 1998. "Fundamental Tax Reform and Corporate Financial Policy." In *Tax Policy and the Economy*, vol. 12, edited by James M. Poterba. Cambridge: MIT Press.

Gokhale, J., B. Page, and J. Sturrock. 1999. "Generational Accounts for the United States: An Update." In *Generational Accounting around the World,* edited by Alan J. Auerbach, Laurence J. Kotlikoff, and Willie Leibfritz. Chicago: University of Chicago Press.

Graetz, Michael J. 1997. *The Decline (and Fall?) of the Income Tax.* New York: W. W. Norton.

Gramlich, Edward M. 1989. "Budget Deficits and National Saving: Are Politicians Exogenous?" *Journal of Economic Perspectives* 3.

Hall, Robert E., and Alvin Rabushka. 1983. *Low Tax, Simple Tax, Flat Tax.* New York: McGraw Hill.

————. 1995. *The Flat Tax*, 2d ed. Stanford: Hoover Institution Press.

Hausman, J. 1981. "Income and Payroll Tax Policy and Labor Supply." In *The Supply-Side Effects of Economic Policy*, edited by L. Meyer. St. Louis: Federal Reserve Bank.

Haveman, Robert. 1994. "Should Generational Accounts Replace Public Budgets and Deficits?" *Journal of Economic Perspectives* 8.

Hubbard, R. Glenn. 1997a. "How Different Are Consumption and Income Taxes?" *American Economic Review* 87 (May).

————. 1997b. *Money, the Financial System, and the Economy*, 2d ed. Reading: Addison-Wesley-Longman.

Kotlikoff, Laurence J. 1992. *Generational Accounting: Knowing Who Pays, and When, for What We Spend.* New York: Free Press.

————. 1993. "From Deficit Delusion to Fiscal Balance Rule—Looking for a Sensible Rule to Measure Fiscal Policy." *Journal of Economics*, supp. 7, pp. 17–41.

Shaviro, Daniel. 1997. *Do Deficits Matter?* Chicago: University of Chicago Press.

U.S. Department of the Treasury. 1992. *Integrating the Corporate and Personal Income Taxes: Taxing Business Income Once.* Washington, D.C.: Government Printing Office.

U.S. General Accounting Office. 1998. "Budget Issues: Long-Term Fiscal Outlook." Statement of Paul L. Posner before the Committee on the Budget, U.S. Senate. Washington, D.C.: GAO.

U.S. Office of Management and Budget. 1997. *Report to Congress on the Costs and Benefits of Federal Regulations.* Washington, D.C.: Government Printing Office.

————. 1998a. *Analytical Perspectives, Budget of the United States Government, Fiscal Year 1999.* Washington, D.C.: Government Printing Office.

————. 1998b. *Draft Report to Congress on the Costs and Benefits of Federal Regulations.* Washington, D.C.: OMB.

About the Authors

KEVIN A. HASSETT is a resident scholar at the American Enterprise Institute. He was a senior economist at the Board of Governors of the Federal Reserve System and an associate professor of economics at the Graduate School of Business, Columbia University. Mr. Hassett was a policy consultant to the Treasury Department during the Bush and the Clinton administrations.

His work in identifying the effects of government policies on business investment behavior has strongly supported the view that the current structure of corporate taxation significantly reduces capital formation and economic growth.

Mr. Hassett has written for the *Quarterly Journal of Economics, Journal of Public Economics,* and other professional journals. He has also contributed to *Investor's Business Daily, Wall Street Journal,* and *Weekly Standard.*

R. GLENN HUBBARD is the Russell L. Carson Professor of Economics and Finance of the Graduate School of Business and the Department of Economics at Columbia University. He is also a visiting scholar at the American Enterprise Institute and a research associate at the National Bureau of Economic Research. He was a visiting professor at the University of Chicago and Harvard University and a John M. Olin Fellow at NBER.

Mr. Hubbard was the deputy assistant secretary of tax analysis at the Treasury Department during the Bush administration. He has been a consultant for the Federal Reserve Board, Federal Reserve Bank of New York, Internal Revenue Service, Social Security Administration, U.S. International Trade Commission, National Science Foundation, and World Bank.

He has written numerous articles on public finance, financial economics, macroeconomics, industrial organization, energy economics, and public policy.